# Haberdasher's Daughter

# *Haberdasher's Daughter*

Poems by

Suzanne Levine

*[signature]*

Antrim House
Simsbury, Connecticut

Copyright © 2010 by Suzanne Levine

Except for short selections reprinted for purposes of
book review, all reproduction rights are reserved.
Requests for permission to replicate should
be addressed to the publisher.

Library of Congress Control Number: 2010927475

ISBN: 978-0-9843418-2-5

Printed & bound by United Graphics, Inc.

First Edition, 2010

Cover design by Peter Good

Author photo by Amy Bloom-Coleman

Book design by Rennie McQuilkin

Antrim House
860.217.0023
AntrimHouse@comcast.net
www.AntrimHouseBooks.com
21 Goodrich Road, Simsbury, CT 06070

In memory of Jack Myers,

who taught me the craft and the Texas two-step

# Acknowledgments

The author wishes to thank the editors of the following publications where poems in this volume originally appeared, sometimes in earlier versions:

*Bellingham Review:* "News" (as "I'd Forgotten about the Lamb")
*California Quarterly:* "Glove Making in Rome"
*Calliope:* "How She Sees Herself"
*The 2009 Chaffin Journal:* "Scents of My Mother," "Saturdays, 1950"
*Permafrost:* "Carnival, Hopewell Junction" (as "Hopewell Junction"), "Little Jack Lake"
*Quiddity International Literary Journal:* "Recipe for the Lonely"
*Stand Magazine (UK):* "I'm Washing Dishes"
*Tendril:* "À la Carte"
*Whiskey Island Magazine:* "Diptych"

Thanks also to the many people who have given me encouragement and to whom I am much in debt: the talented teachers at Vermont College who saw me through my MFA, in particular Roger Weingarten, the director of the program and my mentor for many years; Mark Doty for his attention to every word; and Jill Rosser, whose insights into *Haberdasher's Daughter* as a manuscript were invaluable.

Thanks to Rennie McQuilkin of Antrim House for patience with my word-parsing and insecurities; to Peter Good for his splendid cover design; and to Lary Bloom for the privilege of having him as my editor, mentor and life partner.

None of this would have been possible without my friends and family, especially my parents, Hank and Tops Miller.

# Table of Contents

### TEXTURES

*Heirloom / 3*
*At Eight / 4*
*Miss Jarrell / 5*
*Catching Mother / 6*
*Simple Signs / 7*
*Saturdays, 1950 / 8*
*Posed / 10*
*How She Sees Herself / 12*
*Carnival, Hopewell Junction / 13*
*In Dad's Shop, He Cradles Bolts / 15*
*Problem / 16*
*The Summer of Shorty Pajamas / 17*
*Bamboo Rules / 18*
*Haberdasher's Daughter / 19*
*Crossing, 1964 / 22*

### MEASUREMENTS

*Scents of My Mother / 27*
*News / 30*
*I'm Washing Dishes / 31*
*His Five Minutes / 33*
*Diptych / 35*

## ALTERATIONS

*I Wanted To Tell You* / 39
*Recipe for the Lonely* / 41
*Little Jack Lake* / 43
*NYC Vita* / 45
*Waters* / 47
*À la Carte* / 49
*Last Night a Star Hovered* / 50
*Glove Making in Rome* / 52

## ABOUT THE AUTHOR / 55

**hab.er.dash.er**

*a dealer in men's furnishings & sewing articles
such as buttons & ribbons
early 14$^{th}$C
from Anglo-Fr. "hapertas"
possibly related to "haversack"*

**Heirloom**

It's not the photographs yellowing, or the decades
turning to generations like an alchemist's
fast one—it's the brass

Parisian dancer on her marble
base, one leg aloft in a can-can
number, cast in the '30s. Her metallic

skirt, a pearly
Art Deco sheen, can be lifted to reveal
her shiny V. As a kid visiting

Grandmother, giddy with my first
taste of the forbidden, I raised that
skirt a thousand times—whenever

she went to scatter
crumbs for the pigeons pecking
her kitchen window.

**At Eight**

I'm fully seduced by the TV's gray-and-white
flicker in the form of Oral Roberts on the edge
of a chair receiving the sick and crippled with
*the word of the Lord in my mouth*. Awful

tears and terrible pain seemed to grip
his being—and with no
air-conditioning, sweat poured
over him while his wadded-

up handkerchief hardly helped.
Fiery shouts, tearing
at clothes, and flailing arms all mixed up.
I believed

with Mrs. Valentine,
our sitter. We saw the blind see, the crippled
drop their canes, while she wound
my straight-as-a-stick hair around

the soft leather twists
I'd sleep on and the miracle
of morning curls.

## Miss Jarrell

Under schoolhouse eaves, Calypso,
Cyclops, and Greek
gods, thick with treachery

and deceit, sucked the air
out of the little room where Miss Jarrell
taught spelling demons

until *duly, truly, argument,
ninth,* and *judgment* never
saw an *e* and *parallel*

always had *all*
in its center. Better
than soap opera, Odysseus'

tears and anguish crushed
seventh grade hearts wanting
more. She beat

grammar into the most
stubborn heads with living
clauses, intransitive verbs, and

prepositions as matter, drilled HOMES
for the lakes—Huron, Ontario, Michigan,
Erie and Superior—into memory. *Forget*

*about my gray stockings, slack
at my ankles, sturdy Oxfords*

*on my feet. Remember
demons and the lie-u-ten-ants.*

## Catching Mother

One blustery afternoon
she swayed like a Chinese girl
on bound feet, trying to corral

cotton sheets that snapped
on the clothesline. Wrapping
slender arms around the whites,

she buried her face
in their billowing. A softer
breeze brushed hair

off her forehead and pinked
color on her cheeks as she came
toward the house, the fresh

stack of laundry clasped
safely to her breasts. I swear
I never saw her so happy.

**Simple Signs**

These days it's the promise
of *homemade* that pulls
me over on my doughnut search. But only
ones powdered in gossamer

and light as baby's breath—when
the center's soft
as a fontanel and pulsing
with real raspberry. Only then

do I waken in childhood summers
to Dad's Ford *woody*
pulling into the driveway,
churning stones and crushed clam

shells up to the hubcaps. He waves
a sugar doughnut at us, the passenger's
seat crowded with waxed bakery
bags of hermit cookies and black-

and-whites. Even with rolled-
up sleeves, his shirt is sealed
against his skin in the heat. When
the screen door slams, Mom

pours cold milk
into the cow pitcher and says
to no one in particular
*It looks like a scorcher to me.*

## Saturdays, 1950

By the time Grandfather finished off
his kippers, scrambled eggs and four
slices of Tikotsky's rye, the clock pushed

eleven. Bare-chested, in a steamy
bathroom the hour before, he made paste,
dipping wet bristles into the well

of powdered Pepsodent in his palm. Stupefied
by the ritual, I stood in the foggy
doorway, a small mascot, sweetened

by cologne slapped over his cheeks. After he tucked
the watch fob into his vest, a grey
feathered fedora in one hand, cane

in the other, we drove to the Owl
Shoppe for Connecticut wrapper
cigars. One block over, Maxine,

a buxom red-head, buffed
then polished his nails. At
the factory, thick rubbery

clouds wormed
through our clothes before we reached
his office. Self-inflating rafts fell off

the assembly lines, seven
days a week—those sturdy rafts were all
that stood between our fly boys

and a watery grave. In Hopewell
he rowed our flotilla across
the duck pond through a flock

of mallards, light
years from engagement.

**Posed**

Bachrach himself arranges me
in front of the family
spinet, where my mother's portrait,
probably commissioned,

is centered precisely
between the Viennese sconces,
where she oversees the sitting. His
watch slides on his wrist

when he half
turns my torso, bright in lamb white,
a complement to the dull
Steinway. A tilt

to my head
so dark, mascaraed lashes brush
the apples of my cheeks
as I consider the bouquet

of pale posies. He catches
me there, melting my feet
into a blur of tulle and swirled
netting, like a helpless eddy,

through lens's
trickery. Elegant in black
gabardine, he composes
soft chiaroscuros with hand-

held lights. Out
of upswept hair, my mother's
veil and words cascade
to my shoulders. *All*

*you have to manage, dear,*
*is to endure*
*as I endured.* I'm studying
the sconces, each harvest

fruit painted
on its stem just below
the dangling
crystal teardrops, begging

to be set in motion.

## How She Sees Herself

At thirteen, mirrors
are indispensable. She
opts for the dormer's

opaque window reflection
and rolls an eye
in any direction that casts

a shadow shade of her.
She is everything. All
that is invariably her

makes life explosive
or dull, depending
on which side

of thirteen. She is
every moment
weighing the enormity

of becoming, and sure
no one gives a damn
about a girl at thirteen.

## Carnival, Hopewell Junction

Inside the arched entrance, a velvet
silt kicked up between my toes,
darkening the tops. I remember tucking
the white sleeveless

blouse into rolled-up jeans, cinched by a fake
turquoise belt, as night became
day under lights skimming a humid
blanket of stars that stretched across

all of Dutchess County. Wooden
milk bottles stood at attention in flag-
covered booths waiting
to be knocked silly

with a softball pitch. For a nickel,
would-be sharpshooters unloaded
pop guns at ducks in a row
then dug into their overalls

for another chance. Whirligig
music rose from the carousel
then settled like the pink
cotton candy melting

on my tongue. A parking lot
disguised as thrill
and temptation drew me
night after night toward

the seedy underbelly
of hobos fresh
off freight trains that shook
our house to the root

cellar, like the lies
I told my parents.
Once, I lit a sparkler and waved
crazy eights in the air. One of them

laughed, flicked his cigarette butt into
the dark and led me to the rides.
Afraid of wetting my pants, I held
myself when the ferris wheel

cranked backwards to the top.
Our seat teetered then flung
us to the sky. One hand casual
around my shoulders, his other

replaced my hand and held me *down
there* as the ride skimmed
the hay-strewn ground around
and around again.

## In Dad's Shop, He Cradles Bolts

of camel hair and
cashmere, tames
the matter unfurling

to the floor. With sharp
pins held in his teeth
and a small shard
of soap, he sketches

his language onto me,
multiplied in triple mirrors. The treadle
of a sewing machine slows
when the tailor looks up to read

the crosshatching. *Maybe
next week, the first
fitting*, he tells me. Months
later, October's
brilliance claps my shoulder
but the pattern's off, the fabric,
scratchy. Each fall these blinding

days fold in on another
season of alterations I fail
to make while the Day
of Atonement passes. When

will I be ready to know
markings or codes outside
the contours of a winter coat?

## Problem

Some nights after dinner
Dad put four
quarters on the table

while I stood willing
my brain to know *if
one is removed how

many are left, in percentage
and fraction with reference
to the whole* to please this

persistent father whose lightly
starched cuffs were still
buttoned, whose iris-

blue eyes beseeched my own
to make him proud. I wished
with all my might

he was holding
me like he did when we flew
down the snowy

hills at Elizabeth Park,
Dad steering us
with his feet, riding the Flexible

Flyer like a bucking
bronco, all the way
to the long, smooth run-out.

## The Summer of Shorty Pajamas

Puckered cotton, perfect for nights
when the air hung
curtains around my bed. When the August

of my thirteenth year melted
road tar, I'd roll wads between
fingers and chew until my blackened

tongue told on me. Mother
and I were bull's-eyes
for the sun after rubbing

lotion over our bodies, brown
as berries. Her reach
stretched past sight itself until

the night Dad had one
too many with a business
crony. When I came to kiss

him good night in the pajamas
with tiny bluebells and thin
strip of lace edging

the neckline, Dad lifted
up my top—voilà,
like it was magic: *Look,*

*look at our Susan.*

**Bamboo Rules**


My backyard looks like a movie
set for an old-time jungle
flick, where sharpened bamboo

spearheads, just beneath palm
fronds, wait for the bad guy.
Neighbors gawk

at the fully erect penis
look-alikes that grow three
inches while I sleep—reminders

of the pimples that plagued my teens—crisscrossing
Connecticut for dermatologists after an asshole
boy said, *Jesus, don't you ever*

*wash,* or the crushing *Your face
looks like garbage,* from Dad. Although
Mom's stare-down set him

otherwise, I guessed
he saw his own youth
in my misery—saw another

punch he couldn't take.

## Haberdasher's Daughter

1.

Tips from my father:
*eye contact, kids—always*

*a firm shake—repeat*
*the name, nice*

*to meet you Mr. So*
*and So. Big smile—*

*now he's primed, ready*
*for the pitch.* My brother

in his bookstore works
a customer, tries

to follow Dad's advice
but, unable to hide

disdain, openly
mocks the man copying

titles to order later
on Amazon. Dad replayed

his days each night
between sips

of Johnnie Walker Red
balanced on the worn

arm of his over-
stuffed chair. Only

at home did he rail *That
Yankee cheapskate wants*

*it all for nothing,
nothing, I tell you. Ten*

*God damn years he had the suit.
Comes in complaining*

*a button fell off.* In the shop,
when Dad settled fine Shetland

jackets across the shoulders
of bank and insurance presidents,

he followed his own advice—
locking eyes he'd say *This*

*just came in from Aberdeen.
Do yourself a favor, try*

*it on. You'll feel
like a million bucks.*

2.

*I used to be
a haberdasher. You know,
clothier—dressed*

*the best.* Like a private
joke, Dad's come-on
always came with a kind

of chuckle as his tongue
poked out his cheek, before
the smart flip

of the collar to show *I really
do know fashion.* When
the Grill Room's velvet

gin lined his throat he'd pump
the closest hand and launch
the spiel like an ocean

liner. South Florida's full
of these gentle men. Lucky
for them they travel

in schools telling
and retelling
their story until

it's worn to a shine
like an old blue blazer.

## Crossing 1964

In harbor, the *HMS Elizabeth*
was frightening in size. When I called her
a boat, Mrs. B corrected me: *We
are on a ship, and a damn*

*good one at that.* While high school
myths had me hooked
on heroes' impossible odds, I walked
the gangplank, flanked by my new

husband and in-laws, each holding stiff
leather cases monogrammed in a trio
of letters. My trousseau
gowns wrapped in tissue

were chosen for the formal
dining with captain and first
mate. A watchful
Mrs. B. cautioned

against the three D's—Death,
Divorce and Disaster—banned in polite
company as I spread Russian
caviar on toast points, raised a pink

lipstick-rimmed flute, fizzy with Cliquot,
and clinked mute
hellos to the black
tie and mink-draped

crowd. An on-board squash
court allowed father and son, emotions
suppressed before birth, to aggress
until one, beaten

and nullified, offered a gentleman's
handshake to reset
the rules. For this family, kisses
were pecks and bodies braced

against hugs. The ship's
pool for guessing the distance covered
each day created another fraught
contest before afternoon

bracers of steaming
bouillon. In the writing
salon, fountain
pens thick with ink

and small piles of blue
aerograms were stacked for
travelers eager to scribble
on paper stained with the Queen's

watermark. Having mastered
the letter's folding directions, I chose
instead to shout through static
for a transatlantic

birthday call to Mother—*a miracle
of science*, she marveled. Day 3, storm
clouds enshrouded me, QE's
stabilizers irresolute, as

seasick I heaved, certain
I'd never
make it through *the roughest
crossing on record*—nor ever

know what this maiden
voyage would yield.

# Measurements

# Scents of My Mother

1.

Launched in '27, *Bellodgia's* oriental
stew of cloves, jasmine and lilies, like God's
pillar of cloud that guided a nascent

Israel through the wilderness, was Mother's
inescapable scent that settled
above our lives

like a divination, fine
as powder. Lanolin, for butter-
soft skin, a cake of black

mascara with a tiny brush to spit on
and red-as-rubies lipstick cluttered
the bureau scarf stiffly running over

the edges
of her mahogany dresser. Ironing
Dad's shirt,

she drove the snarling nose
into a cuff. *I've got cancer,*
she said through the steam

that hissed a starched, almost
burnt bouquet
into the room.

2.

I held her hand all the way to the public
beach, a barefoot seven-
year-old growing so fast my bathing

suit climbed up my bottom, tan
as the rest of me. A town pass
on their Cadillac window, my grandparents

drove the quarter mile in style. With rocks
for drying salty suits and waterlogged life
jackets, we camped—spreading towels, folding

chairs, a wicker hamper and army
blankets, marking our spot. Endless
hands of gin

kept Grandmother and Auntie at each other's
throats until—rubberized
in bathing slippers and caps, synchronizing

backstrokes toward the wharf—they
cooled off. A disciple
of water and sun, Mother believed each

pilgrimage to this seaweed-
strewn shore would cure
her cancer. She painted her browned

body with long strokes of cocoa
butter that knocked
me drowsy like when we'd drive

early to the Hometown
Bakery to watch doughy ladies shake
powdered sugar over dozens

of doughnuts, turning
the air to confection.

## News

Dad always held back
the screen door with an elbow, a loaf
of bread from Lantieri's

under his arm,
and leaned into the steamy
kitchen for her kiss. That was the way

he came home that July night,
except there was no
bread under his arm, his tie

wasn't quite right, and only
one foot was in
the kitchen, the other strangely

outside, while he bent
against the screen
as if he couldn't bear the weight

of the news he broke—*We lost
Mom*. I don't remember
anything after, except we tried

to eat something, Dad made
a lot of calls, and the house grew
empty with strangers.

**I'm Washing Dishes**


when an ambulance backs into Mrs.
Harwood's drive. EMTs
hurry a folding
stretcher through the kitchen
like last time when the siren's
blast and red

strobes woke me after midnight. For months
round-the-clock nurses sidestepped
an African violet left outside to fend
for itself, the old Federal house still
a grand dame despite the sunken
roofline and obvious shortcuts

by shyster carpenters and locals
passing themselves off as handy. When the end
comes, I don't really notice until garbage
bags and boxes of clothes begin to pile against

vinyl siding and a fuzzy
cardigan lies matted on the grass. Mrs. Harwood's
son and his wife lift a dining table
with claws for feet into a U-Haul while their kids

run in and out of the converted chicken
coop and up to the rocky end of her
yard. Tag sale
signs go up and most folks
in the village come for a look-see. Portable
potties, walkers, and crutches propped

against ashtrays from Montreal
and Savannah take over
her sunroom. Used
tinsel, glass candy
canes and dented tin peacocks hang
next to papery wreaths

signed in a child's hand. I never met
Mrs. Harwood and try to look
beyond the soured breath
of the dingy rooms. A table

of unmatched china and chipped
tea cups takes me back
to Hopewell Junction where
Grandmother drank tea

with teaspoons of plum
jelly and sipped from saucers when shaky
hands rattled cups. Decades of
smoking eventually
killed her but not before she wound
her dreams like a tea bag

around a spoon and squeezed
every ounce of flavor
into her *waste not,*
*want not* world.

**His Five Minutes**

In spite of the suffocating
humidity, guarded,
gated communities and miles

of strip malls serving retirees
bad Thai, to keep from going
stir crazy, I cook Dad

his favorites—Mom's
whipped cream chocolate
roll or apple brown betty, even her five-

minute egg with a buttery
side of rye, a twenty-
four-hour antidote in the limbo

of reprieve, but always too
runny under my step
mother's impatience. With each

visit, he disappears into his challis robe's
tissue lightness, and dresses
less and less. One morning

on his bed's edge
in the unfamiliar
briefs that Ursula

prefers, his hands knead
the tattersall spread, his shoulders
rounding as he weeps, folding

in on himself. Never
brave—we once
moved because, while he was lost

in the paper and coffee, a snapping
turtle wandered into our yard. He feared
death, being the last of six

boys, the baby, babied throughout—
craving child's pap, while counting
the minutes down.

# Diptych

## January Orange

When I cut the last orange
into sections, they teeter

on the small blue plate like dinghies
tied at the pier. A chapter,

as they say, has ended with a phone
call, something I think over

while sucking the life
out of the feather-weight

pulp, tear-shaped and sheer
as silk, and I know now

there is nothing ordinary
in this world.

## Shoe Dreams

Sometimes I recognize the arch
of a foot when shadows

take shape. Once
Dad's wing tip swung

out of the dark
into light and back again

as though keeping tempo
with a tune only

he could hear. Mother's
lizard pump has a habit

of showing up, dangling from
a nylon toe when her strand

of pearls, lustrous with age
encircles my neck.

*Alterations*

## I Wanted to Tell You

about the cardinal's blacker-
than-coal beak against
his breast, dressed
orangine in this light, how
he lit upon the pear's muscled
branch with forsythia
busting yellow heads
beyond. You didn't
get it—truly, you couldn't
conjure up this scene
in front of your
distracted eyes, even
if everything
you cared about
depended on it. Instead

of a breakdown, I light
the gas and warm
waves of pale oil.
At six I hear the door
open in triumph.
Your thumb slits envelopes—
a paper flurry in the hall—
and your briefcase thuds to
its corner home. Then a light
tap to the paperweight and small
photograph on the desk to reset
symmetry, wild trumpets
of amaryllis and zealous

paperwhites just this
side of too sweet, unnoticed.

I peel, chop, quarter, cube
then mix native
vegetables and purple
basil into the large
speckled bowl. An unwieldy
onion rings my finger but angry
tears fall free.

Even this
ratatouille built from yellow
peppers and cherry
tomatoes turns opaque.

## Recipe for the Lonely

He doesn't believe you—
and never will. Hang
up the phone. Open

the Montrachet into his
gift of handblown
glass. Slip Art

Tatum into the CD
changer, then blanch
green beans,

smash fat
garlic cloves into virgin
olive oil, warming. So he

thinks you dissed
his daughter when she
came east. Remove

when golden, add hot
red flakes and *fuck you
Seattle* to crispy pancetta,

raise the heat until
you cool down, season
with coarsely

ground pepper. Chop
the hell out of a fistful
of parsley and dress

your best plate
as "Humoresque" breaks
into arpeggios.

## Little Jack Lake


In the north Kawarthas, a half
day from here, walleye,
muskie, and steelhead beg
to be fried over an open

fire just off the porch of a friend's
cottage she calls *the sweetest place
on Earth*. And now that you are lost
to me, I need that promise

of the falls, those Biblical
waters of lustration, to lighten
my body, soaked from the miles
I've walked, unable to be still. Maybe

her neighbor is skilled, when sober, at excising
pain. Maybe a limb, maybe
two, will have to go. I'll trust
his judgment way up north,

where even the cough
syrup gets him high. Maybe
we'll just shoot the shit, but it's
possible we'll fuck or

fall in love—unlikely
but maybe—when I get to
Little Jack Lake and try
to forget how my breath

caught when you returned a wisp
of hair behind my ear. The little
death in each of those grand,
small moments.

## NYC Vita

"The only color we have left is *Rain*," the shop
girl tells me, wrapping the dress in noiseless

tissue, "but, it's stunning with your
*tobacco* shoes." She leans close

and whispers, *"Rush*, I know
your scent, it's *Rush"*—louder now

as I leave, checking
once over my shoulder to make

sure she's not coming to expose
me for just another

sucker seduced by any
slick package. A bus plastered

with an ingénue's smile sends me
to a CVS for anti-aging

promises in a jar. *Ruby Stain* resists
the back of my hand like a tattoo

turned ugly, weeping into lip lines, a hard
look against *Baby's Face*

brushed over the arcs
of my cheeks. Under my skirt, *Barely*

*There* panties have shifted uncomfortably.
I don't see the young meter maid until

she looks at me as she passes. But
in that moment I see

myself in a loopy grin
forming at the corner

of her pale mouth as she slaps
a hot pink ticket under the blade.

**Waters**

After removing all traces
of artifice—mother's silver

rings, a circle
of gold, and the clear

polish I've worn
for decades—I step

into the *mikvah*. Three
times I dive into the ritual

bath, lifting my feet
off the bottom, and remember

rainbow brookies grandmother
cast for early

mornings—the sacramental
hooking, then release, back

into the creek. Her lacquered
nails a Chinese

red, brilliant against
their underbellies

in the feisty
current. Always

the angler, she depended
on men—much as the trout

depend on water
striders and mayflies. Traveling

light, choosing escapade
over her only child,

she could be counted
on for carelessness and dark

beauty—part American
Indian—just one

of her courted
lies. Before cancer's final run

over my mother, two
women who'd never

even washed their own hair closed
the bathroom door each

afternoon and opened
the taps to the healing waters.

## À la Carte

How can I make a poem for you
when all I think about is crushing
slivered almonds while heating
elliptical globes of garlic that bring
you to your knees with their urgency?
Heady now from the rush, I toast
bread crumbs with curls of parsley.
You hold mushroom caps on the swelling
of your palm and gently press
stuffing into crevices, crown
the flutings until full. We sprinkle
cheese, spritz with pale
wine, bake until bronzed. It helps
to have a concentration
of the right ingredients. Take,
for instance, a nice
Jewish boy and a half
Jewish girl with mother-in-law who swears
that food is love.

## Last Night a Star Hovered

above the gibbous moon,
slightly to the right of its
hump. Sky
watchers call it
El Nath, Arabic

for "the butting one,"
and place it smack
at the tip of Taurus,
the bull, claiming
it packs a shine more

luminous than the sun. More
is made of the fact
that El Nath sits precisely
opposite the nucleus
of our galaxy. Important

stuff, I think, not
the sticky stuff
of children up to their grimy
elbows in God
knows what. Wide awake

and firmly embedded, I slip
my arm under
yours and fold
my need
to be irreplaceable against

you—one of two
cusps, well-suited
for a moon
on the run.

## Glove Making In Rome

With the soft underside of my arm
in one hand, he cradled my elbow
into a pillow of green

velvet and set my upper
arm at a right angle
semaphore. Samples

of pigskin, suede, and calf,
in small piles on his worktable, smelled
faintly of rough play, the working

and reworking of skin. He guided
the glove's creamy fingers over
rings, swelling leather,

and deeper still, into each valley
of my willing hand. In one
elegant thrust he palmed my hand, pressing

both sides of the glove to my wrist. *Grazie,
mille grazie*, I managed, but for what,
I wasn't sure, and would not know until our fingers

first interlocked and I remembered that
moment in Italy and the true
weight of measurement and dimension, the sheer

wonderment of fit and sweet
bindings that tether us.

Photo by Amy Bloom-Coleman

Suzanne Levine was born in Poughkeepsie, New York, and is a long-time resident of Connecticut. Her work has appeared or is forthcoming in *Bellingham Review*, *California Quarterly*, *Calliope*, *Permafrost*, *Quiddity International Literary Journal*, *Interpoezia*, *Southern California Review*, *Whiskey Island Magazine*, and other publications. A Pushcart nominee, she was a finalist in the 2009 Midnight Sun Chapbook Competition and a contributor to *Forty Fathers* (2009). Suzanne holds an MFA from Vermont College and teaches the craft of memoir writing with Lary Bloom at the Mark Twain House in Hartford, as well as Connecticut libraries and community centers. She lives in Chester, near her children and grandchildren. You can visit her website at www.suzannelevine.net.

This book is set in Garamond Premier Pro, which had its genesis in 1988 when type-designer Robert Slimbach visited the Plantin-Moretus Museum in Antwerp, Belgium, to study its collection of Claude Garamond's metal punches and typefaces. During the mid-fifteen hundreds, Garamond — a Parisian punch-cutter — produced a refined array of book types that combined an unprecedented degree of balance and elegance, for centuries standing as the pinnacle of beauty and practicality in type-founding. Slimbach has created an entirely new interpretation based on Garamond's designs and on comparable italics cut by Robert Granjon, Garamond's contemporary.

To order additional copies of this book
or other Antrim House titles, contact the publisher at

Antrim House
21 Goodrich Rd., Simsbury, CT 06070
860.217.0023, AntrimHouse@comcast.net
or the house website (www.AntrimHouseBooks.com).

•

On the house website
are sample poems, upcoming events,
and a "seminar room" featuring supplemental biography,
notes, images, poems, reviews, and
writing suggestions.